HYDROPONICS

The ultimate Guide for the Soilless Grower for vegetables and herbs

4 BOOKS OF 10

BY

Peter Clark

2

Chapter 1. Introduction to Hydroponics

The word hydroponics has its deduction from joining the two Greek words, hydro, which means water, and ponos, which means work (i.e., working water). The word 1st showed up in a science related magazine article distributed in February 1937 and was composed by W. F. Gericke, who had acknowledged this word as was recommended by Dr. W. A. Setchell at the University of California. Dr. Gericke started exploring different avenues regarding hydroponics developing procedures in the last part of the 1920s and afterward distributed one of the early books on soilless developing. Later he recommended that the capacity to create yields would at this point don't be "tied to the dirt however certain business harvests could be filled in bigger amounts without soil in bowls containing arrangements of plant food." What Dr. Gericke neglected to anticipate was that hydroponics becoming would be basically restricted to encased conditions for developing high money esteem crops and would not discover its way into the creation of a wide scope of monetarily developed yields in an open climate.

1.1 What is Hydroponics?

I went to three word references and three reference books to discover how hydroponics is explained. Webster's New World College Dictionary, fourth edition,1999, explains hydroponics as "the study of developing or the creation of plants in supplement rich arrangements or soggy idle material, rather than soil"; the Random House Webster's College Dictionary,1999, as "the development of plants by putting the roots in fluid supplement arrangements as opposed to in soils; soil less development of plants"; and the Oxford English Dictionary, second release, 1989, as "the way toward developing plants without soil, in beds of sand, rock, or comparative supporting material submerged with supplement arrangements. "In the Encyclopedia Americana, worldwide release, 2000, hydroponics is explained as "the act of developing plants in fluid supplement societies instead of in soil"; in the New Encyclopedia Britannica, 1997, as "the development of plants in supplement improved water with or without the mechanical help of an inactive medium, like sand or rock"; and in the World Book Encyclopedia, 1996, as "the study of developing plants without soil". The most well-known part of every one of these explanations is that hydroponics methods developing plants without soil, with the wellsprings of supplement components as either a supplement arrangement or supplement enhanced water; an idle mechanical root support (sand or rock) might be utilized. It is fascinating to take note of that in just two of the six explanations is hydroponics explained as a "science." Searching for explanations of hydroponics in different books and articles, coming up next were found. Devries explains hydroponics plant culture as "one in which all supplements are provided to the plant through the water system water, with the developing substrate being soilless (generally inorganic), and that the plant is developed to create blossom or organic products that are collected available to be purchased." likewise, he states, Hydroponics used to be viewed as a framework where there was no developing media by any means, for example, the Nutrient Film Technique in vegetables. In any case, today it's acknowledged that a soilless developing medium is frequently used to help the plant root framework truly and accommodate a great cushion of arrangement around the root framework. Resh explains hydroponics as "the study of developing plants without the utilization of soil, however by utilization of an idle medium, like rock ,sand, peat, vermiculite, pumice, or sawdust, to which is added a supplement arrangement containing every one of the fundamental components required by the plant for its typical development and improvement." Wignarajah explains hydroponics as "the method of developing plants without soil, in a fluid culture." In an American Vegetable Grower article named, "Is Hydroponics the Answer?" hydroponics was explained with the end goal of the article as "any strategy which utilizes a supplement arrangement on vegetable plants, developing with or without unnatural soil mediums". Harris recommended that a cutting edge explanation of hydroponics would be "the study of developing plants in a medium, other than soil, utilizing combinations of the fundamental plant supplement components disintegrated in water." Jensen expressed that hydroponics "is an innovation for developing plants in supplement arrangements (water containing composts) with or without the utilization of an unnatural medium (sand, rock, vermiculite, rockwool, perlite, peat greenery, coir, or sawdust) to offer mechanical help." furthermore, Jensen explained the developing of plants without media as "fluid hydroponics" and with media as "total hydroponics." Similarly related hydroponics terms are "water) culture," "hydro-culture," "nutriculture," "soilless culture," "soilless agribusiness," "hydroponics," or "synthetic culture." A hydroponicist is explained as one who rehearses hydroponics, and hydroponicum explained as a structure or gar-lair in which hydroponics is drilled. In reality, hydroponics is just one type of soilless culture. It alludes to a method wherein plant establishes are suspended in either a static, ceaselessly circulated air through supplement arrangement or in a constant course or fog of supplement arrangement. The developing of plants in an inorganic substance (like sand, rock, perlite, or rockwool) or in a natural material, (for example, sphagnum peat greenery, pine bark, or coconut thread) that are intermittently watered with a supplement arrangement ought to be alluded to as soilless culture however not really hydroponics. Some may contend with these explanations, as the normal origination of hydroponics is that plants are developed without soil, with 16 of the 19 required fundamental components given through a supplement arrangement that occasionally washes the roots. The greater part of the books on hydroponics society center around the overall culture of plants and the plan of the developing framework, giving just crude subtleties on the establishing bed plan and the creation and the executives of the supplement arrangement. Albeit the techniques for arrangement conveyance and plant support media may change significantly among hydroponics frameworks, most have demonstrated to be functional, bringing about sensibly great plant development.

In any case, there is a notable distinction between a "working framework" and one that is economically suitable. Tragically, numerous useful soilless culture frameworks are not monetarily practical. Most books on hydroponics would persuade that hydroponics society techniques for plant developing are moderately liberated from issues since the establishing media and supply of supplement components can be controlled. Jensen, in his outline, expressed, "Hydroponics society is an innately appealing, frequently over simple innovation, which is far simpler to elevate than to support. Sadly, disappointments far dwarf the triumphs, because of the executive's inability or absence of science and designing help." Experience has shown that hydroponics developing requires cautious consideration regarding subtleties and great developing abilities. Most hydroponics developing frameworks are difficult to oversee by the unpracticed and incompetent. Soil developing is more for-giving of blunders made by the producer than are most hydroponics developing frameworks, especially those that are absolutely hydroponics.

1.2 Is Hydroponics a Science?

This inquiry has been habitually posed without an explicit answer. Most word references don't explain hydroponics as a science, but instead as another methods for developing or developing plants. In any case, the Webster's New World College Dictionary, fourth release (1999), does explain hydroponics as "the study of developing or the creation of plants in a supplement rich arrangement." I would expect that the science viewpoint is that related with "in a supplement rich arrangement." Not even in the Wikipedia explanation and going with portrayal of hydroponics does "science" show up. Presumably the lone association effectively occupied with the science viewpoint is the National Aeronautic Space Administration (NASA) since some type of hydroponics will be the chosen technique for developing plants in space or on heavenly bodies. The Merriam Webster's Collegiate Dictionary's explanation for science is "something (as a game or technique) that might be considered or educated like arranged information."

Hydroponics is without a doubt a procedure for developing plants and there has amassed a collection of information in regards to how to develop plants utilizing a hydroponics technique (or should it be the hydroponics strategy?), subsequently suitable-chime the rule for being a "science" in light of the former explanation. Additionally, there is an amassed assortment of "systemized information" that suits the second piece of the science explanation.

1.3 Hydroponic Terminology

Likewise with each specialized subject, there fosters a language, just as a language, that gets acknowledged by those exploring and applying that innovation. Notwithstanding, the created language or potentially language can be con-intertwining to those new to the innovation, and now and again in any event, for those inside. Accordingly, the hydroponics writing can be confounding to per users because of the assortment of words and terms utilized. The words "hydroponics" and "soilless" cultivator have are as yet being utilized to allude to a similar strategy for developing, however in this content "hydroponics" is utilized when developing frameworks are simply hydroponics that is, there is no establishing medium or the establishing medium is considered idle. "Soilless" is utilized for frameworks of developing that identify with plant creation in which the medium can cooperate with plant roots, for example, natural substances like peat greenery and pine bark. In the naturally based creating plant science innovation, there are two words that are often utilized: food and supplement.

It very well may be befuddling if these words are not plainly explained and perceived. What came into regular use, starting during the 1950s, was the word food to recognize a synthetic compost, a substance that contains one or cut off. Today in both agronomic and agricultural writing, it isn't extraordinary to recognize a NPK (nitrogen, phosphorus, potassium) compost as plant food, a word blend that has been for the most part acknowledged and generally utilized and comprehended. One word reference explanation of food identified with plants is "inorganic substances consumed by plants in vaporous structure or in water arrangement". This word reference explanation would be in concurrence with the word blend plant food, since synthetic manures are inorganic and root assimilation of the components in a substance compost happens in a water arrangement climate. Consequently, the words food and additionally plant food would not identify with naturally based substances for use as compost since these two terms have effectively been explained to distinguish inorganic substances. Along these lines, those natural substances for use as a compost ought to be recognized by name instead of as either a food or plant food.

The word supplement is obscure in its significance and utilized in various science related departments. A word reference explanation doesn't help as it isn't certain, being explained as "a nutritive substance or fixing." For plant nourishment application, supplement is perceived as being one of the thirteen plant fundamental mineral components that have been separated into two classifications: the six significant mineral components N, P, K, Ca, Mg, and S found at percent focuses in the plant dry matter, and the seven micronutrients B, Cl, Cu, Fe, Mn, Mo, and Zn found in the dry matter of the plant at under 100% levels. For assigning one of the thirteen plant fundamental mineral components, the term plant supplement component is oftentimes utilized, for example, expressing that P is a fundamental plant supplement component. Utilizing the term supplement component doesn't give the appropriate recognition as that being related with plants. Shockingly, the phrasing utilized in both science related and specialized plant diaries has been messy in recognition of the fundamental plant mineral components, alluding to them as fundamental supplements, plant supplements, or simply the word supplement. For those occupied with the plant sciences, most by and large comprehend what these terms mean, however for somebody not all that drew in, the word supplement could have importance for a wide scope of substances as being "a nutritive substance or fixing." In the naturally based plant developing language, the word supplement is utilized as a comprehensive term that additionally incorporates natural mixtures containing consolidated and fortified carbon, hydrogen, and oxygen. In this manner, one may ask, "What is the contrast between a plant mineral component and a substance recognized as a supplement that is a natural substance?" This inquiry is hard to reply since the standards for building up vitality for the plant mineral components have been as of now settled, while rules of centrality for other than a mineral component have not. Along these lines, similarly as with the utilization of the words food or plant food, the utilization of the word supplement ought to be restricted to the recognition of just a plant fundamental mineral component; those recommending plant nutritive incentive for a natural substance should utilize just the word for that substance and not recognize it as a supplement.

1.4 Historical Past

The developing of plants in plant supplement component rich water has been drilled for quite a long time. For instance, the antiquated Hanging Gardens of Babylon and the buoyant nurseries of the Aztecs in Mexico were hydroponics in nature. During the 1800s, the fundamental ideas for the hydroponics developing of plants were set up by those examining how plants develop. The soilless culture of plants was then promoted during the 1930s in a progression of distributions by a California researcher. During the Second World War, the US Army set up enormous hydroponics nurseries on a few islands in the western to supply new vegetables to troops working around there. Since the 1980s, the hydroponics procedure has come into business use for vegetable and blossom creation, with more than 86,000 sections of land of nursery vegetables being developed hydroponically all through the world a grounds that is relied upon to keep on expanding. One of the parts of hydroponics that has impact its conventions is the way that the hydroponics procedure for developing plants is utilized principally in controlled conditions, like nurseries, where the air encompassing plants and its temperature, stickiness, and development are controlled. Indeed, even the effect of sunlight based radiation is fairly controlled (altered) by the transmission qualities of the nursery coating. Consequently, those providing details regarding their utilization of a special hydroponics strategy are mentioning observable facts that are the aftereffect of the association between the plant climate and developing procedure, regardless of whether it be a swamp-and-channel, NFT, or dribble water system technique with plants established in rockwool or coir chunks, or cans of per-light. At that point the inquiry concerns the worth of data being accounted for when plants are filled in a glass nursery situated in the mountains of Arizona utilizing the rockwool chunk trickle water system framework for somebody who might be considering developing a similar plant animal types in a twofold polyethylene-shrouded nursery situated in the beach front fields of south Georgia (United States) utilizing the rockwool piece dribble water system developing strategy. Quite a long while prior, I made successive visits to four hydroponics producers, one situated in Georgia and three in South Carolina. All were developing tomatoes in twofold layered polyethylene-shrouded Quonset-type green-houses, with the tomato plants established in perlite-pervade BATO pails utilizing a dribble water system framework for conveying a supplement arrangement. I immediately discovered that the ability of these cultivators was a central point influencing their acquired yield and natural product quality. All were following the operational methods given by the provider of the nursery and hydroponics developing framework. Every cultivator had encountered a few occasions of plant supplement component lack, and thus, one had rolled out a significant improvement in the supplement arrangement explanation he was at initial utilizing. All were doing genuinely well as far as organic product yield and quality, albeit extra experience would presumably have brought about an improvement in both. In the accompanying developing season things changed: Both organic product yield and quality declined, as totally attempted to change their operational systems to adapt to what was happening, yet without progress. One producer finished his yield in middle of the season; the other three looked for a response to why things had changed asking me at each visit just as settling on wild phone decisions to the individuals who had prompted them in the past when managing different issues. Albeit no particular circumstances and logical results was uncovered, climate conditions had changed noteworthy that year: The colder time of year and spring months were hotter than typical, and there were less overcast days with extremely dry cools, with low precipitation prompting dry spell conditions in the whole region.

From climate station information, the minutes of daylight during this timeframe were greatly higher than in earlier years. From these information I reasoned that the radiation contribution to their nurseries was greatly higher than in past seasons, in this way focusing on the plants, with the outcome being low natural product yield and helpless natural product quality (generally little fruit).What may have aided would have been drawing conceal material over the plant overhang during the high early afternoon times of extreme radiation. Likewise required was an adjustment of the supplement arrangement plan just as managing the times of water system to decrease the pressure that was happening with the aggregation of "salts" in the perlite. Also, carrying molded air into the nursery up through the plant shelter would have kept the plant foliage cooler and added to reliable support of plant leaf bloat. Could these methodology be then considered "systemized information" and, whenever known and applied, would they have forestalled the organic product misfortunes these cultivators experienced? From the time that the Hoagland/Arnon supplement arrangement plans were presented, little exploration has been committed to researching the utilization of these two details under different application approaches. It isn't exceptional to peruse an article in an exploration diary or specialized distribution in which the essayist utilizes the expression "altered Hoagland supplement arrangement" without demonstrating whether the actual explanation was adjusted or one of its utilization boundaries. The utilization boundaries given by Hoagland and Arnon were 1 gallon of supplement arrangement per plant with substitution every week. Accordingly, what impact on plant development would happen on the off chance that one of these boundaries were changed? Another great inquiry. From one ought genuine experience, the study of hydroponics to be explained dependent on going with natural conditions; that one bunch of hydroponics developing methods would just apply to a special arrangement of developing boundaries and along these lines not a secure set of strategies that would apply generally. Until this is perceived, the utilization of the hydroponics strategy for developing will struggle in a labyrinth of deception; cultivators will be continually looking for answers to why things occurred as they managed without uncovering the reason, and the individuals who need to realize the reason will be searching for an answer in every one of some unacceptable spots. Appropriate guidance in the plan and operations of a hydroponics society framework is significant. Those curious about the potential dangers related with these frameworks or who neglect to comprehend the science of the supplement arrangement needed for their appropriate administration and plant sustenance will neglect to make business progress with most hydroponics society frameworks. The innovation related with hydroponics plant creation has changed little as can be seen by assessing the different catalogs on hydroponics. Today, those inspired by hydroponics look for data from sites on the Internet. The test isn't absence of information (there are more than 400,000 hydroponics sites), but instead the swamping of data, much inadequate with regards to a science related premise, that prompts disarray and helpless dynamic with respect to clients." Is Hydroponics the Answer?" was the title of an article that showed up in 1978 that contained comments by those conspicuous around then in the hydroponics industry. In the article was the accompanying statement: "Hydroponics is inquisitively delayed to get the mass producer underwriting that some imagined at one time." Later, Carruthers gave a potential response to what had been happening in the United States, expressing that "the purposes behind this lethargic development can be credited to numerous components, including a wealth of rich, fruitful soil and a lot of clean water." At the 1985 Hydroponics Worldwide: State of the Art in Soilless Crop Production gathering, Savage expressed in his survey that "numerous extreme cases have been made for hydroponics/soilless frameworks, and numerous guarantees have been made too early, yet actually a gifted cultivator can accomplish wondrous outcomes." also, Savage saw "soilless culture innovation as having reached 'adulthood' and fast developing to follow," further expressing that "soilless and controlled climate crop creation takes extraordinary abilities and preparing; in any case, most disappointments were not the consequence of the developing strategy, but rather can be ascribed to poor monetary arranging, the executives, and advertising." At the 2003 South Soilless Culture Conference, Alexander covered flow advancements, expressing that "hydroponics is developing quickly all over and inside the following 5 to 10 years will be set up as a significant piece of our agrarian and agricultural creation ventures." His forecast presently can't seem to work out. Prior, Wilcox expounded on the "High Hopes of Hydroponics," expressing that "future accomplishment in the nursery business will request smallest expense, different trimming creation procedures closer to the significant populace habitats." In 1983, Collins and Jensen arranged an outline of the hydroponics method of plant creation, and Jensen talked about plausible future hydroponics improvements, expressing that "the future development of controlled climate horticulture will rely upon the advancement of creation frameworks that are cutthroat as far as expenses and gets back with open department agribusiness," and that "the fate of hydroponics shows up more sure today than any

16

time in the course of the most recent 30 years." In a concise audit of hydroponics developing exercises in Australia, Canada, England, France, and Holland, Brooke expressed that "the present hydroponics rancher can develop crops securely and in places that were in the past thought to be too infertile to even consider developing, like deserts, the Arctic, and surprisingly in space." He finished up, "Hydroponics innovation traverses the globe." Those searching for a brief outline of the regular frameworks of hydroponics filling being used today will search the article by Rorabaugh accommodating.

Naegely expressed that the "nursery vegetable business is blasting." She finished up, "The following quite a long while guarantee to be a powerful time in the nursery vegetable industry." Growth in the hydroponics nursery industry was extensive during the 1990s, and it's proceeded with future extension will rely upon advancements that will keep "controlled natural horticulture" (CEA) frameworks monetary advantageous. Jensen commented that "while hydroponics and environment con-savaged agribusiness (CCA) are not equivalent, CEA generally goes with hydroponics their possibilities and issues are inseparable." "Hydroponics for the New Millennium: A Special Section on the Future of the Hydroponic Industry" is the title of a progression of articles by six patrons who tended to this point from their own viewpoints; the last remark was, "It truly is an energizing opportunity to be in the overall hydroponics industry, regardless of whether it's for business creation or a pastime". Jones and Gibson expressed that "the fate of the proceeded with development of hydroponics for the business supportive of duct of plants isn't empowering except if a significant advancement happens in the manner the procedure is planned and utilized." Those elements restricting wide application, composed Jones and Gibson, "are cost, the prerequisite for solid electrical force, inabilities in the utilization of water and supplement components, and natural necessities for removal of spent supplement arrangement and developing media." Schmitz commented that "hydroponics is additionally seen as excessively specialized, excessively costly, too everything. "It ought to be noticed that these remarks in regards to hydroponics were composed preceding 2000, considering the perspectives from a wide range of sources. Since 2000, little has been expounded on hydroponics as far as its benefits and impediments, and there have been no noteworthy propels that have diverted its application.

1.5 The Future of Hydroponics

Resh addresses the eventual fate of hydroponics by expressing that, "in a moderately brief timeframe, over around 65 years, hydroponics has adjusted to numerous circumstances from open air department culture and indoor nursery culture to exceptionally special culture in the space program." He likewise expresses that the lone restrictions for the utilization of hydroponics developing would be "water and supplements." also, Resh sees numerous future uses of hydroponics in an assortment of circumstances, from food creation in desert districts to metropolitan and space applications. What isn't empowering for what's to come is the absence of contribution from researchers in open rural schools and examination stations that at one time made noteworthy commitments to trim creation methods, including hydroponics. The early hydroponics analysts, Dr. W. F. Gericke and D. R. Hoagland, for instance, were employees at the University of California, a land-award college. Today, a couple in comparative colleges are as yet dynamic in hydroponics examinations and exploration. The current status of rural agreeable expansion programs shifts extensively from one state to another. Previously, state subject matter experts and area specialists assumed significant parts as hotspots for solid data, however today these administrations are being scaled back. Likewise, not many of these trained professionals and specialists have any ability in hydroponics or broad involvement with managing nursery the board issues. Edwards, nonetheless, saw a positive job that region expansion workplace play in giving help to those looking for data when he composed that "the Extension workplace is frequently the initial place these individuals contact." The study of hydroponics is at present little explored, and a large part of the current spotlight is on the use of existing hydroponics methods. Hydroponics, as a strategy for developing, is by and large basically sup-ported by those in the private area who have a personal stake in its financial advancement dependent on the items that they market. Another upsetting variable is that the Hydroponic Society of America has not been dynamic since 1997, when it distributed its last Proceedings.

The general public was established in 1979 and had been holding yearly gatherings and distributing procedures from 1981 through 1997. Additionally, the International Society of Soilless Culture, an association that had held gatherings and distributed procedures previously, has not been dynamic for quite a while. The job that business and science related progressions have on society can't be overlooked while thinking about the thing is happening in hydroponics today. The simplicity of development of produce by surface and air transport, for instance, considers developing food items at huge spans from their place of utilization. The coming of plastics massively affects hydroponics since developing vessels, fluid stockpiling tanks, dribble water system tubing and connections, nursery coating materials, and sheeting materials fundamental parts in all hydroponics/nursery activities are gotten from a wide scope of plastic materials that change in their physical and compound attributes. The utilization of PCs and PC control of essentially every part of a hydroponics/nursery activity has changed dynamic and administrative control methods. Albeit one may reason that hydroponics yield creation is turning out to be increasingly more a science, there is still a lot of craftsmanship necessitated that makes this strategy for plant creation a test just as an undertaking.

1.6 Hydroponic Practice and the Art of Hydroponics

Any individual who wishes to try hydroponics has prepared admittance to every one of the assets that are should have been fruitful and can develop plants utilizing one of the different hydroponics developing frameworks with great outcomes. The test is to take those equivalent assets and create the most noteworthy plant yield and quality. Strolling into any nursery where plants are being developed hydroponically, I can rapidly survey the nature of the board expertise being applied, the consequence of applying novel abilities that a few people appear to have that capacity to take a bunch of operational boundaries and make them work viably and workable together. I'm one who hardly accepts that there are people who have what is known as a "green thumb," while there are other people who do well with the assets they have, however appear to remain at a degree of execution underneath those with a "green thumb." It is like the individuals who can prepare a delectable feast, while another person utilizing similar data sources can create a connoisseur supper.

1.7 Value of the Hydroponic Method

In 1981, Jensen recorded the benefits and impediments of the hydroponics procedure for crop creation, large numbers of which are as yet appropriate today:

Advantages

• Crops can be developed where no reasonable soil exists or where the dirt is sullied with sickness.

• Labor for plowing, developing, treating, watering, and other customary practices is to a great extent dispensed with.

• Maximum yields are conceivable, making the framework financially achievable in high thickness and costly land territories.

• Conservation of water and supplements is a component, everything being equal. This can prompt a decrease in

20

contamination of land and streams since significant synthetics need not be lost.

• Soil-borne plant sicknesses are all the more promptly killed in shut frameworks, which can be absolutely swamping with an eradicant.

• More unlimited oversight of the climate is by and large an element of the framework (i.e., root climate, convenient supplement taking care of, or water system), and in nursery type tasks, the light, temperature, dampness, and organization of the air can be controlled.

• Water conveying high dissolvable salts might be utilized whenever finished with outrageous consideration. In the event that the solvent salt focuses in the water sup-employ are more than 500 ppm, an open arrangement of hydroponics might be utilized if care is given to visit draining of the developing medium to lessen the salt aggregations.

• The novice horticulturist can adjust a hydroponics framework to home and porch type gardens, even in elevated structures. A hydroponics framework can be spotless, lightweight, and motorized.

Disadvantages

• The initial development cost per section of land is incredible.

• Trained staff should coordinate the developing activity. Information on how plants develop and of the standards of sustenance is significant.

• Introduced soil-borne infections and nematodes might be spread rapidly to all beds on a similar supplement tank of a shut framework.

• Most accessible plant assortments adjusted to controlled developing conditions will require innovative work.

• The response of the plant to great or helpless sustenance is unimaginably quick. The cultivator should notice the plants each day.

Wignarajah gave the accompanying benefits of hydroponics over soil developing:

• All of the supplements provided are promptly accessible to the plant.

• Lower groupings of the supplement can be utilized.

• The pH of the supplement arrangement can be controlled to guarantee ideal supplement take-up.

• There are no misfortunes of supplements because of filtering.

Wignarajah gave just one impediment of hydroponics frameworks: "that any decrease in the oxygen strain of the supplement arrangement can make an anoxic condition which hinders particle take-up." His suggestion is that just aeroponics tackles this issue since it gives a "prepared inventory of oxygen to the roots, thus never gets anoxic."

1.8 Internet and Units of Measure
The job of the Internet has changed and will keep on changing how society instructs itself. One can get the data and gadgets expected to build up and deal with a hydroponics developing framework off the Internet. However, the Internet is "inundated" with endless hydroponics sites, and the test is the way to isolate what is solid and valid from that which isn't correct or dependable while swimming through the mass of material that exists.

The hydroponics writing can be befuddling to users because of the assortment of words and terms utilized just as a blend of British and metric units. In this book, when needed to explain the content, both British and metric units are given.

Chapter 2. How Plants Grow?

The old scholars pondered about how plants develop. They inferred that plants acquired sustenance from the dirt, considering it a "special juyce" existent in the dirt for use by plants. In the sixteenth century, van Helmont viewed water as the sole supplement for plants. He reached this resolution in the wake of leading the accompanying test: Growing a willow in an enormous painstakingly gauged tub of soil, van Helmont saw toward the finish of the test that lone 2 ounces of soil was lost during the time of the test, while the willow expanded in weight from 5 to 169 pounds. Since just water was added to the dirt, he presumed that plant development was created exclusively by water. Later in the sixteenth century, John Woodward developed spearmint in different sorts of water and saw that development expanded with expanding debasement of the water. He reasoned that plant development expanded in water that contained expanding measures of earthbound matter, since this matter is abandoned in the plant as water goes through the plant. The possibility that dirt water conveyed "food" for plants and that plants "live off the dirt" overwhelmed the thinking about the occasions. It was not until the mid-to late eighteenth century that experimenters started plainly to see how, in reality, plants develop. At about a similar time, the "humus" hypothesis of plant development was proposed and was broadly acknowledged. The idea proposed that plants acquire carbon (C) and fundamental supplements (components) from soil humus. This was presumably the main idea of what might today be known as the "natural (cultivating)" idea of plant development and prosperity. Analyses and perceptions made by numerous individuals from that point forward have limited the fundamental reason of the "humus hypothesis" that plant wellbeing comes just from soil humus sources.

2.1 Photosynthesis

Joseph Priestley's celebrated trial in 1775 with a creature and a mint plant encased in a similar vessel set up the way that plants will "cleanse" as opposed to exhaust the air, as do creatures. His outcomes opened a totally different space of examination. 25 years after the fact, DeSaussure established that plants burn-through carbon dioxide from the air and delivery oxygen when in the light. Hence, the interaction that we today call "photosynthesis" was found, in spite of the fact that it was not surely known by DeSaussure or other sat that time. The interaction of photosynthesis is the change of sun based energy into compound energy within the sight of chlorophyll and light.

A water atom taken up through the roots is parted and afterward the hydrogen partition is joined with a particle of carbon dioxide from the air that has passed into an open stoma to frame a sugar, and in the process an atom of oxygen is delivered. The pace of photosynthesis is influenced by factors outer to the plant, for example, air temperature (high and low), air development over the leaf surfaces, level of carbon dioxide noticeable all around the leaves, light force and its frequency arrangement, and water status in the plant. Photosynthesis happens essentially in green (chlorophyll-containing) leaves, since they have stomata, and not in the other green parts (petioles and stems) of the plant, which don't have stomata. The quantity of stomata on the leaves and whether they are open or shut will likewise influence the pace of photosynthesis. Bloated leaves in a ceaseless move of air and with open stomata will have the most elevated photosynthetic rate.

2.2 Soil Fertility Factors

In the nineteenth century, an experimenter named Boussingault started to notice plants cautiously, estimating their development in various kinds of treated soil. This was the start of numerous trials showing that the dirt could be controlled through the expansion of fertilizers and different synthetic substances to influence plant development and yield .However, these perceptions didn't disclose why plants reacted to changing soil conditions. At that point came an acclaimed report in 1840 by Liebig, who expressed that plants get all their carbon (C) from carbon dioxide noticeable all around and the mineral components by root retention from the dirt. Another time of getting plants and how they become arisen. For the initial time, it was perceived that plants use substances in both the dirt and the air. Resulting endeavors went to recognizing those substances in soil, or added to soil, that would enhance plant development in wanted ways. The worth and impact of special synthetic substances and excrements on plant development took on new importance. The department tests led by Lawesand Gilbert at Rothamsted (England) prompted the idea that substances other than the actual dirt can impact plant development. About this time, the water tests directed by Knop and other plant physiologists (a background marked by how the hydroponics idea was imagined is given by Steiner 1985) showed decisively that K, Mg, Ca, Fe, and P, alongside S, C, N, H, and O, are largely essential for vegetation. It is fascinating to see that the recipe conceived by Knop for developing plants in a supplement arrangement can be utilized effectively today for application in most hydroponics developing frameworks.

Remember that the mid-nineteenth century was a period of extraordinary science related disclosure. The specialists named before are nevertheless a couple of the individuals who made noteworthy revelations that impact the reasoning and course of science related natural examination. Large numbers of the noteworthy disclosures of that day fixated on organic frameworks, both plant and creature. Prior to the turn of the nineteenth century, the science related premise of plant development had been grounded, as has been explored by Russell. Specialists had demonstrated definitively that plants get carbon (C), hydrogen (H), and oxygen (O) needed for carb amalgamation from carbon dioxide and water by the cycle called photosynthesis; that N was gotten by root retention of ammonium as well as nitrate particles (albeit leguminous plants can enhance this with cooperatively attached nitrogen from the air); and that the wide range of various components are taken up by plant roots from the establishing medium as particles and moved all through the plant being conveyed in the happening stream. This overall framework remains today as the reason for our present under-remaining of plant capacities. We currently realize that 16 components (C, H, O, S, N, P, K, Ca, Mg, B, Cl, Cu, Fe, Mn, Mo, and Zn) are fundamental for typical plant development.

We have broadened our insight about how these components work in plants; at what levels they are needed to keep up sound, lively development; and how the components other than C, H, and O are root assimilated and moved inside the plant. Despite the fact that there is a lot of that we do think about plants and how they develop, there is still a lot of that we don't altogether see, especially about the part of a portion of the fundamental components. Equilibrium, the connection boat of one component to another or among the components, and natural structure might be pretty much as significant as the centralization of any of the components in advancing the plant's wholesome status. There is still some vulnerability concerning how components are consumed by plant roots and how they at that point move inside the plant. Natural structure, regardless of whether singular particles or buildings, might be as significant for development and use as focus. For instance, chelated iron (Fe) structures are successful for control of Fe shortage, despite the fact that un-chelated ionic Fe, either as ferric or ferrous particles, might be similarly powerful yet at higher fixations. The naturally dynamic segment of a component in the plant, often alluded to as the labile structure, might be that bit of the focus that decides the personality of plant development. Instances of these labile structures would be the nitrate type of N, the sulfate type of S, and solvent segment of Fe and Ca in plant tissue types of these components that decide their excess status. The idea and utilization of plant examination (here and there alluded to as tissue testing) are mostly founded on this idea of estimating that part of the component that is found in the plant tissue or its sap, and afterward relating that focus to plant development.

The study of plant sustenance is pulling in extensive consideration today as plant physiologists decide how plants use the fundamental components. Moreover, the attributes of plants would now be able to be hereditarily controlled by adding or potentially eliminating characteristics that modify the capacity of the plant to withstand natural pressure and improve item quality. With these numerous advances, all types of developing, regardless of whether hydroponics or something else, are currently getting more useful. A lot of this work is being accomplished for developing plants in space and correspondingly constricted conditions where the information sources should be painstakingly controlled because of restricted assets, like water, and control of the arrival of water fume and other unpredictable mixtures into the air around the plant. A large part of things to come of hydroponics may lie with the advancement of plant cultivars and cross breeds that will react to exact control of the developing climate. The capacity of plants to use water and the fundamental components adeptly may make hydroponics techniques better than what is conceivable today.

2.3 The Plant Root

Plant roots have two significant capacities:

• Physically anchor the plant to the developing medium

• Act as a road through which water and particles go into the plant for rearrangement to all pieces of the plant.

Albeit the initial job given here is significant, it is the second job that merits our consideration in this conversation. The book altered via Carson gives definite data on plant roots and their numerous significant capacities, and the book part by Wignarajah examines the mutt lease ideas on supplement component take-up. Root engineering is controlled by plant species and the actual climate encompassing the roots. Plant roots develop outward and down-ward. Notwithstanding, in soil, it has been seen that feeder digs grow up, not down. This is the reason plants, especially trees, do inadequately when the dirt surface is compacted or actually upset. In soil, any root limitation can affect plant development and advancement because of the decrease in soil–root contact. Root pruning, regardless of whether done deliberately (to bonsai plants) or as the consequence of characteristic marvels (because of the presence of furrow or dirt dish), will likewise influence plant development and advancement in soil. In most hydroponics developing frameworks, roots may stretch out into a lot more noteworthy volume of developing territory or medium than would happen in soil. Root size, estimated as far as length and degree of stretching just as shading, is a trademark that is influenced by the idea of the establishing climate. Regularly, enthusiastic plant development is related with long, white, and exceptionally stretched roots. It is dubious whether vivacious top development is a consequence of energetic root development or the other way around. Tops will in general develop to the detriment of roots, with root development easing back during organic product set. Shoot-to-root proportions are as often as possible used to portray the relationship that exists between them, with proportions going from as low as 0.5 to a high of 15.0. Root development is reliant upon the inventory of carbohydrates from the tops and, thusly, the top is subject to the root for water and the necessary fundamental components. The misfortune or limitation of roots can noteworthy influence top development. Consequently, it is accepted that the objective ought to be to give and keep up those conditions that advance great, sound root improvement, neither unnecessary nor prohibitive. The actual attributes of the actual root assume a significant part in basic take-up. The establishing medium and the components in the medium will decide to an extensive degree root appearance. For instance, root hairs will be practically missing on attaches presented to a high fixation (100mg/L, ppm) of nitrate. High P in the establishing medium will likewise decrease root hair advancement, while changing centralizations of the significant cations, potassium, calcium, magnesium will have little impact on root hair improvement. Root hairs particularly increment the surface accessible for particle ingestion and furthermore increment the surface contact among roots and the water mist around particles in a soilless medium; along these lines, their essence can markedly affect water and particle take-up. Regularly, hydroponics plant roots don't have root hairs. The inquiry that emerges is, "The thing that comprises solid working roots for the hydroponics developing framework?" The size and degree of root improvement are not as basic as in soil. It has been shown that one working root is adequate to give every one of the fundamental components needed by the plant, with size and breadth of the roots being basically significant for water take-up. Thusly, in most hydroponics frameworks, root development and expansion are likely far more prominent than required, which may really detrimentally affect plant development and execution. It ought to be recalled that root development and capacity require a persistent stockpile of starches, which are created by photosynthesis. Subsequently, an always extending and effectively working root framework will remove starches from vegetative development and organic product development. Consequently, some level of root development control might be fundamental for broad plant development and high organic product yields. An enormous and broad root framework may not be the awesome most hydroponics developing frameworks. Maybe than the huge root mass, dynamic, adeptly working roots are required, since the supplement arrangement constantly washes the majority of the root framework, accordingly requiring less surface region for retention to happen. One of the serious issues with the NFT (Nutrient Film Technique) tomato hydroponics framework, for instance, is the huge root mass that creates in the establishing channel, which at last limits oxygen and supplement arrangement infiltration; the outcome is an issue called "root demise." Similar broad root development happens with different sorts of developing frameworks, especially with swamp-and-channel frameworks, where roots habitually develop into the funneling that conveys and depletes the developing bed of supplement arrangement, confining even move. Comparative broad root development is gotten with most hydroponics frameworks with roots every now and again padding packs and squares of media; likewise, in some cases roots develop through the openings in the external dividers of sacks and media holders. The inquiry is, "Does a huge root mass convert into high plant execution?" The appropriate response is likely no if there is more root surface for assimilation than required. Moreover, roots require a constant inventory of starches, which can be better used to extend top development and add to natural product yield. A huge root mass likewise requires significant amounts of oxygen to remain completely useful. Shockingly, the inquiry as to attach size still can't seem to be tended to adequacy. It ought to likewise be recollected that roots require a persistent inventory of oxygen to stay sound and working. Roots won't make due in anaerobic conditions. Hydroponically talking, a huge, always extending root framework presumably doesn't really convert into more prominent top development and yield and, truth be told, may really have some negative impact.

2.4 Water Content and Uptake

The state of the plant is dictated by its water content, for when the water content decreases, shriveling happens and the plant starts to lose its shape and starts to hang. Shriveling happens at initial in recently creating tissue that has not yet fostered a hard cell structure. There might be conditions where water take-up and development inside the plant are inadequate to keep the plant completely bloated, especially when the air request is high and additionally when the establishing climate (temperature, air circulation, and water and saltiness levels) is to such an extent that it confines the take-up of water through the roots. All in all, department-developed plants are less delicate to water pressure than are plants filled in controlled conditions, which may halfway clarify why plants in the nursery are especially touchy to water pressure, which thusly noteworthy impacts development rate and advancement. Water is in a real sense pulled up the conductive tissue (basically in the xylem) by the deficiency of water from the leaves of the plant by a cycle called "happening," which happens predominantly through open stomata situated on leaf surfaces just as lenticels and the cuticle are also used.

To comprehend this cycle, imagine a persistent section of water from the root cells up to climatically uncovered leaves; the pace of water development is driven by a water possible inclination between the leaves and the encompassing air. Happening has two significant impacts: It decreases foliage temperature by evaporative cooling (as plant leaves assimilate sun oriented energy, the vast majority of the consumed energy is changed over into warmth), and it gives the actual power to the movement of components from the digging climate up into the upper bits of the plant. Leaves presented to coordinate sun oriented radiation will ascend in temperature if water development up the plant is limited. Leaf temperature influences paces of photosynthesis, breath, and plant development. The measure of water lost by happening will rely upon the distinction in fume pressure between the leaf and encompassing air. Leaf and air temperatures sway gas diffusional rates; henceforth, paces of photosynthesis and leaf breathe all reduction with expanding leaf temperature. The pace of happening increments with expanding development of air over the leaf surfaces at comparable stomata gap openings. Also, water lost by happening is dictated by a mind boggling relationship that exists between air temperature and relative dampness just as the ordered categorization and ontogenetic age of the plant organ. With the end goal for water to enter the roots, the roots should be completely useful. Water retention by plant roots decays with diminishing temperature, diminishes with expanding particle substance of the water encompassing the root, and diminishes with diminishing oxygen substance of the encompassing root mass climate. Temperature is another significant factor that impact root development, just as the assimilation of water and fundamental component particles. The ideal root temperature will differ to some degree with plant species, however by and large, root temperatures underneath 68°F (20°C) start to achieve changes in root development and conduct. Beneath the ideal temperature, there are diminished development and expanding, prompting coarser looking root frameworks. Ingestion of both water and particles is likewise eased back as the porousness of cell layers and root energy are diminished with diminishing temperature. Movement all through the root is similarly eased back at not exactly ideal root temperatures (68° F to 86° F [20° C to 30° C]). At the point when root temperatures are underneath the ideal (just as being not exactly the air temperature), plants will shrivel during high air request periods, and basic lack will show up. Particle retention of the components P, Fe, and Mn is by all accounts more influenced by low temperature than that of a large portion of the other fundamental components, major, and micronutrients. It ought to likewise be noticed that the consistency of water diminishes with diminishing temperature, which thusly influences water development in and around the plant root. The most extreme root temperature that can be endured before decrease in root action happens isn't unmistakably known. Roots appear to have the option to endure brief times of high temperature. Roots are completely practical at 86° F (30° C) and presumably can withstand temperatures up to 95° F (35° C). In any case, the current writing isn't clear regarding the special furthest reaches of the ideal temperature range for best plant development. To keep away from the perils of one or the other low or high temperatures, the roots and establishing medium ought to be kept at a temperature somewhere in the range of 68°F and 86°F (somewhere in the range of 20°C and 30°C). Diminished development and different side effects of helpless nourishment will show up if root temperatures are kept at levels underneath or over this suggested temperature range. Air circulation is another significant factor that impact root and plant development. Oxygen is fundamental for cell development and capacity. If not benefit capable in the establishing medium, extreme plant injury or passing will happen. The energy needed for root development and particle assimilation is determined by the cycle called "breath," which requires oxygen. Without satisfactory oxygen to help breath, water and particle retention stop and roots pass on. Oxygen levels and pore space conveyance in the establishing medium will likewise influence the improvement of root hairs. High-impact conditions, with equivalent appropriations of water- and air-consumed pore spaces, advance root development, including root hair improvement. On the off chance that air trade between the medium and encompassing air is hindered by overwatering, or the pore space is diminished by compaction, the oxygen supply is restricted and root development and capacity will be unfavorably influenced. When in doubt, if the pore space of a strong medium, such assoil, sand, rock, or a natural blend containing peat greenery or pine bark, is similarly involved by water and air, excess oxygen will be available for ordinary root development and capacity. In hydroponics frameworks where plant establishes are filling in a standing arrangement or a move of supplement arrangement, the producer is confronted with "Impasse" issue in times of high temperature. The solvency of oxygen in water is very low (at 75° F, about 0.004%) and diminishes greatly with expanding temperature, as is outlined. Be that as it may, since plant breath, and in this way oxygen interest, increment quickly with expanding temperature, regard for oxygen supply is required. In this manner, the supplement arrangement should be kept all around circulated air through by either gurgling air or oxygen into the arrangement or by uncovering however much of the outside of the arrangement as could be expected to air by unsettling. One of the great benefits of the aeroponic framework is that plant establishes are basically filling in air and subsequently are by and large satisfactorily provided with oxygen consistently. Root passing, a typical issue in most NFT frameworks and perhaps other developing frameworks also, is expected to a limited extent to absence of excess air circulation inside the root mass in the establishing channel. In soil and soilless establishing media, a more noteworthy root mass can add to expanding assimilation limit, while in a hydroponics developing framework, root mass is less a contributing element. The wholesome status of a plant can be a factor, as a sound effectively developing plant will supply the required starches needed to support the roots in a functioning respiratory condition. It is by and large accepted that the majority of the water assimilation by plant establishes happens in more youthful tissue simply behind the root tip. Water development across the root cortex happens basically intercellular, yet can likewise happen extracellular with expanding happening rate .As water is maneuvered into the plant roots, those substances break down noise the water will likewise be brought into the plant, albeit a profoundly particular framework manages which particles are conveyed in and which are kept out. Along these lines, as the measure of water retained through plant roots builds, the measure of particles taken into the root will likewise increment, despite the fact that a guideline framework exists. This mostly clarifies why the natural content of the plant can differ contingent upon the pace of water take-up. Hence, climatic interest can be a factor influencing the essential substance of the plant, which can be either good or inconvenient. Likewise, numerous other

35

water-solvent mixtures in the establishing medium may be brought into the plant and enter the xylem.

2.5 Ion Uptake

All fundamental mineral component particles in plant root cells are at a higher con-centration than that present in the general climate. Thusly, how are the mineral component particles ready to move against this fixation slope? Accordingly, Jacoby suggests the accompanying conversation starters: 1. How is entry through the impermeable fluid layer achieved? 2. How is aggregation against the fixation angle achieved? 3. How is metabolic energy coupled to such vehicle? 4. What is the system of selectivity? 5. How is vectorial transport achieved? The responses to the majority of these inquiries still can't seem to be addressed completely. Notwithstanding, the ideas of particle assimilation and development up the plant are depicted by six cycles: 1. Free space and osmotic volume 2. Metabolic vehicle 3. Transport proteins 4. Charge equilibrium and stoichiometry 5. Transport proteins 6. Transport to the shoot. The ingestion of particles by the root is by both a detached and a functioning interaction. Contingent upon the particle, transport is by inactive uniport through channels or via transporter helped co-transport with protons. Aloof root ingestion implies that a particle is conveyed into the root by the section of water; that is, it is somewhat "conveyed" along in the water taken into the plant. It is accepted that the latent method of transport clarifies the high convergences of certain particles, like potassium, nitrate and chlorine found in the stems and leaves of certain plants. The controlling components in inactive retention are the measure of water moving into the plant (which changes with climatic interest), the centralization of these particles in the water encompassing the plant roots, and the size of the root framework. Inactive assimilation isn't the entire story, in any case, as an interaction including substance selectivity happens when a particle bearing arrangement arrives at the root surface. The layers of the root cells structure a powerful boundary to the pas-sage of most particles into the root. Water may move into these cells, however the particles in the water will be abandoned in the water encompassing the root. Additionally, another marvel is grinding away: Ions will just move actually from a space of high fixation to one of lower focus, a cycle known as dissemination. Notwithstanding, on account of root cells, the grouping of most particles in the root is regularly higher than that in the water encompassing the root. Subsequently, particles should move from the root into the encompassing water and, without a doubt, this can and happens. The inquiry is the way particles move against this fixation inclination and enter the root. The appropriate response is by the cycle called "dynamic ingestion."

In a common place plant root, solutes can be found in three compartments. The peripheral compartment, where solutes have prepared availability, is called evident free space (AFS) or external free space (OFS). This compartment contains two sub compartments: water free space (WFS), which broke up sub-positions (like particles) can unreservedly move into by dispersion, and Donnan free space (DFS), whose cell dividers and layers have various stable adversely charged locales that can tie cations. The cation trade limit of plant cells is controlled by the DFS. Particle development across these cell dividers and films requires both energy and a transporter framework. Dynamic assimilation works dependent on transporters and Michaelis–Mentenkinetics. These speculations depend on the idea of cell layers, which work in a few different ways to control the movement of particles from outside to inside the cell. It is entirely expected to discuss "shipping" a particle across the cell layer and, without a doubt, this might be what occurs. A particle might be complex with a special substance (most likely a protein) and afterward "conveyed" across (or through) the film into the cell against the focus inclination. For the framework to work, a transporter should be available and energy consumed. At this point, nobody has had the option to decide the special idea of the transporter or transporters, albeit the transporters are believed to be proteins. Notwithstanding, the transporter idea assists with clarifying what is seen in the development of particles into root cells. The other hypothesis identifies with the presence and capacity of particle or proton siphons as opposed to transporters. For both of these frameworks to work, energy is required: one connected to respiratory energy and the other from adenosine triphosphate (ATP), a high-energy moderate related with most energy-requiring measures. For a more point by point clarification on the instrument of particle take-up by roots, allude to the article by Wignarajah. In spite of the fact that we don't have a clue about the whole clarification for dynamic retention, general arrangement exists that some kind of dynamic framework controls the development of particles into the plant root. We know three things about particle retention by roots:

1. The plant can take up particles especially despite the fact that the external fixation and proportion of components might be very unique in relation to those in the plant. 2. Gathering of particles by the root happens across an extensive con-centration slope. 3. The assimilation of particles by the root requires energy that is produced by cell digestion. A remarkable component of the dynamic arrangement of particle ingestion by plant roots is that it displays particle rivalry, threat, and synergism. The serious impacts confine the assimilation of certain particles for other people. Instances of upgraded take-up connections include:

• Potassium take-up is preferred over calcium and magnesium take-up.

• Chloride, sulfate, and phosphate take-up is animated when nitrate take-up is emphatically discouraged.

The pace of assimilation is likewise extraordinary for different particles. The monovalent ions (i.e., potassium, chlorine, nitrate are more promptly consumed by roots than the divalent (calcium, magnesium, sulfur) particles. The take-up of special particles is additionally improved in dynamic take-up. In the event that the nitrate anion is the significant N source in the encompassing establishing climate, at that point there will in general be an adjusting impact set apart by more prominent admission of the cations potassium, calcium and magnesium cation is the significant wellspring of N, at that point take-up of the cations potassium, calcium and magnesium is decreased. Moreover, the presence of smelling salts improves nitrate take-up. In the event that chlorine particles are available in sizable focuses, nitrate take-up is diminished. These impacts of particle rivalry, hostility, and synergism are of extensive significance to the hydroponics producer to keep away from the danger of making essential awkward nature in the supplement arrangement that will, thus, influence plant development and organic product advancement and yield. Along these lines, the supplement arrangement should be appropriately and painstakingly adjusted at initial and afterward kept in balance during its term of utilization. Lopsided characteristics emerging from these particle impacts will influence plant development. Steiner (1980) has talked about unimportant detail his ideas of particle balance while comprising a supplement arrangement. Sadly, numerous current frameworks of supplement arrangement the executives don't successfully manage the issue of unevenness. This is genuine not just of frameworks in which the supplement arrangement is overseen based on week by week unloading and reconstitution yet additionally of consistent movement of frameworks. Surely, the idea of quick, consistent movement, low-fixation supplement arrangement the executives is made to glance misleadingly encouraging in limiting the collaborating impacts of particles in the supplement arrangement on ingestion and plant sustenance. At long last, non-ionic substances fundamentally atoms disintegrated in the water arrangement encompassing the plant root can likewise be taken into the root by mass movement. Substances like amino acids, straightforward proteins, sugars, and urea can enter the plant and perhaps add to its development and improvement, something that has not been very much reported. Metabolic vehicle across root structures into the xylem vessels controls the quantity of particles passed on to the tops; strangely, the number is minimal influenced by the speed of xylem sap movement. Once in the xylem, particles and other dissolvable solutes move by mass movement, principally to the leaf apoplast.

2.6 Root Surface Chemistry

Many plant attaches can change the climate quickly around their underlying foundations. The most well-known change is a decrease in pH by the discharge of hydrogen particles. Moreover, a few plants can produce substances, (for example, siderophores) from their foundations that improve particle chelation and take-up. These marvels have been most regularly seen in species that can acquire required Fe under antagonistic conditions and are normal for alleged "iron (Fe) - structured" plants. This capacity of roots to modify their quick climate might be hampered in hydroponics frameworks where the pH of the supplement arrangement is as a rule continually changed vertical or in those frameworks where the supplement arrangement isn't reused. In such cases, care should be taken to guarantee that the appropriate equilibrium and supply of the fundamental components are given, since the plant roots will be unable to change the attaching climate to suit a special need. The effect of roots on a standing circulated air through supplement arrangement framework may adversely affect plant development by one or the other raising or bringing down the arrangement pH, just as by the presentation of complex substances into the arrangement. Hence, incessant checking of the supplement arrangement and close perception of plant development and advancement can make the cultivator aware of the supplement arrangement's evolving status.

Chapter 3. The Essential Plant Nutrient Elements

As the years progressed, a bunch of terms has been created to characterize those components fundamental for plant development. This wording can be confounding and deluding to those new to it. Indeed, even the accomplished can get shaken every once in a while. Similarly as with any group of information, an acknowledged language fosters that is seen well exclusively by those effectively occupied with the department. One of the ordinarily abused terms is alluding to the fundamental metallic components, like Cu, Fe, and Zn, as being classed as minerals. The exacting explanation of mineral alludes to a compound of components instead of a solitary component. However, mineral supplement is a usually utilized term when alluding to plant natural sustenance. This expression once in a while shows up related to different words, for example, plant mineral sustenance, mineral nourishment, or plant nourishment all of which allude to the fundamental components and their prerequisites by plants. Another generally abused and misconstrued word is "supplement," alluding again to a fundamental component. It is getting progressively regular to consolidate the words supplement and component to mean a fundamental component. Hence, components, for example, N, P, and K are known as "supplement components." Unfortunately, nobody has proposed a fitting wording when discussing the fundamental components; consequently, the writing on plant nourishment contains a combination of these terms. In this book, "fundamental plant supplement component" is the term utilized instead of supplement component or supplement.

3.1 Terminology

The early plant specialists fostered a bunch of terms to group the 16 elements recognized as fundamental for plants; these terms have gone through changes lately. At initial, the significant components so named on the grounds that they are found in sizable amounts in plant tissues incorporated the components C, H, N, O, P, and K. Shockingly, three of the now named fundamental significant components Ca, Mg, and S were at initial named "auxiliary" components. These purported auxiliary components ought to be classed as significant components, and they are alluded to as such in this content. Those components found in more modest amounts at initial were designated "minor components" or in some cases "minor components" (B, Cl, Cu, Fe, Mn, Mo, and Zn). All the more as of late, these components have been renamed "micronutrients," a term that better suits the similar proportions between the significant components found in sizable fixations and the micronutrients found at lower focuses in plant tissues. Another term that has been utilized to assign a portion of the micronutrients is "substantial metals," which alludes to those components that have generally high nuclear loads. One explanation is "those metals that have a thickness more noteworthy than 50 mg/cm" with components, for example, Cd, Co, Cu, Fe, Pb, Mo, Ni, and Zn being considered as weighty metals. Another classification that has started to advance into the plant sustenance writing is the alleged "good components," which will be discussed later. The normal convergence of the fundamental components in plants is given in utilizing information by Epstein. All the more as of late, Ames and Johnson recorded the significant components by their interior focuses found in higher plants.

Another as of late named class is minor components, which alludes to those components found in plants at extremely low levels (1 ppm) yet not recognized as one or the other fundamental or good. A portion of these minor components are found in the A–Z micronutrient arrangement. The word "accessible" has a special undertone in plant nourishment speech. It alludes to that type of a component that can be consumed by plant roots. In spite of the fact that its utilization has been all the more firmly aligned with soil developing, it has improperly showed up in the hydroponics writing. All together for a component to be taken into the plant, it should be in a solvent structure in the water arrangement encompassing the roots. The accessible structure for most components in arrangement is as a particle. It ought to be called attention to, notwithstanding, that some sub-atomic types of the components can likewise be assimilated. For instance, the atom urea, (a solvent type of N); the boric corrosive particle, H; and some chelated edifices, like Fe DTPA, can be consumed by the plant root.

3.2 Criteria for Essentiality

The standards for centrality were set up by two University of California plant physiologists in a paper distributed in 1939. Arnon and Stout portrayed three necessities that a component needed to meet to be viewed as fundamental for plants:

• Omission of the component being referred to should bring about unusual development, inability to finish the existence cycle, or unexpected passing of the plant.

• The component should be special and not replaceable by another.

• The component should apply its impact straightforwardly on development or digestion as opposed to by some roundabout impact, for example, by estranging another component present at a harmful level. Some plant physiologists feel that the rules set up by Arnonand Stout may have coincidentally adjusted the quantity of fundamental components at the current 16, and that for a long time to come no extra components will be tracked down that meet their rules for centrality. The 16essential components, the pioneer of every component, the pioneer of centrality, and the date of revelation; the 16 fundamental components, the structure used by plants, and their capacity in plants. Some plant physiologists feel that it is just a short time before the vitality of Co, Ni, Si, and V, referred to now as good components, will be illustrated, that those components ought to be added to the current rundown of 16 fundamental plant supplement components, and that they ought to be available in the establishing medium or be added to the attaching medium to guarantee best plant development.

3.3 The Major Elements

Nine of the 16 fundamental components are divided as significant components: C, H, O, N, P, K, Ca, Mg, and S. The initial three are acquired from carbon dioxide noticeable all around and water from the establishing medium and afterward joined by photosynthesis to frame starches through the response carbon dioxide in addition to water (within the sight of light and chlorophyll) carb in addition to oxygen. Accordingly, they are not regularly examined in any detail as novel to hydroponics developing frameworks. The components C, H, and O address about 90% to 95% of the dry load of plants and are in reality the significant constituents. The leftover six significant components, N, P, K, Ca, Mg, and S, are more essential to the hydroponics cultivator since these components should be available in the supplement arrangement in excess fixation and in the legitimate equilibrium to meet the harvest prerequisite. A large portion of the excess 5% to 10% of the dry load of plants is comprised of these six components. An outline of the significant perspectives and attributes of the significant components is found.

3.4 The Micronutrients

Plants require significantly more modest centralizations of the micronutrients than the significant components to support plant supplement component excess. Be that as it may, the micronutrients are however fundamentally fundamental as the significant components may be. The ideal focuses for the micronutrients are ordinarily in the scope of 1/10,000 of the fixation range needed for the significant components. The micronutrients, collectively, are undeniably more basic as far as their control and the board than a portion of the significant components. On account of a few of the micronutrients, the necessary reach is very thin. Takeoff from this tight reach results in either diseased or poisonousness when beneath or above, individually, the ideal fixation range. Diseased or poisonousness manifestations are normally hard to assess outwardly and in this manner require an investigation of the plant for endorsement. A lack of a micronutrient can as a rule be amended effectively and rapidly, however when managing overabundances or poison levels, remedy can be hard, if certainly feasible. On the off chance that poisonousness happens, the cultivator may well need to begin once again. Hence, extraordinary consideration should be taken to

45

guarantee that an abundance convergence of a micronutrient not be brought into the establishing media, either at initial or during the developing season. The accessibility of a portion of the micronutrients, especially Fe, Mn, and Zn, can be greatly changed with an adjustment of pH or with an adjustment of the centralization of one of the significant components, especially P. In this manner, legitimate control of the pH and centralization of the significant components in a supplement arrangement is similarly basic. There might be enough centralization of a portion of the micronutrients in the common habitat (i.e., in the water used to make a supplement arrangement, the inorganic or natural establishing media, or from contact with channeling, stockpiling tanks, and so on) to block the necessity to supply a micronutrient by expansion. Hence, it is ideal to dissect a pre-arranged supplement arrangement in the wake of establishing it and after contact with its current circumstance to decide its micronutrient content. Also, cautious observing of the establishing media and plants will guarantee that the micronutrient prerequisite is being relaxed yet not surpassed. A rundown of the significant angles and qualities of the micronutrients is found.

3.5 Content in Plants

The significant components, C, H, O, N, P, K, Ca, Mg, and S, exist at rate focuses in the plant dry matter, while the micronutrients exist at centralizations of 0.01% or less in the dry matter. To try not to befuddle decimals, micronutrient fixations are communicated in milligrams per kilo-gram (mg/kg) or parts per million (ppm). Different terms are utilized to explain natural focus, yet % and mg/kg will be the terms utilized in this book. A correlation of normally utilized focus units is given. Plant natural substance changes significantly with species, plant part, and phase of development in addition with the impact of level of essential accessibility. Basic substance information are for the most part dependent on dry weight judgments, albeit some component conclusions, like N as nitrate anion), can likewise be made utilizing sap extricated from live tissue. A component may not be equally disseminated among different plant parts (roots, stems, petioles, and leaves), and lopsided circulations may likewise exist inside a leaf and among leaves at different phases of advancement. Knowing the grouping of a component in an indicated plant part at the known phase of development, and surprisingly its appropriation inside the actual plant, can give significant data to explaining the nourishing status of the plant.

Function in Plants

The essential and auxiliary parts of the relative multitude of fundamental components needed by plants are genuinely notable. A few components are constituents of plant compounds (like N and S, which are constituents of proteins); some fill in as chemical activators (K, Mg, Cu, Mo, Zn), have inclusion in energy move responses (P and Fe), are straightforwardly as well as in a roundabout way identified with photosynthesis (Mg, P, and Fe), or fill in as osmotic balancers (K). A few components have basically one job or capacity; other shave various jobs and capacities.

Forms of Utilization

For the entirety of the fundamental components, the structure or types of the component used are ordinarily special as a solitary ionic structure, like potassium, calcium, magnesium, copper, zinc, chlorine; more than one ionic structure.

3.6 The Useful Elements

The quantity of components as of now thought to be fundamental for the legitimate sustenance of higher plants remains at 16; the last component added to that rundown was Chlorine in 1954. Some plant physiologists feel that the measures for centrality set up by Arnon and Stout could block the expansion of different components, as these 16 incorporate a large portion of the components found in generous amounts in plants. In any case, there might be different components that presently can't seem to be demonstrated fundamental, as their necessities are at such low levels that it will take significant complex logical abilities to reveal them, or their pervasive presence will require unique abilities to eliminate them from the attaching medium to make a lack. This was the situation for Cl, the remainder of the fundamental components to be so explained. The inquiry is which components are probably going to be added to the rundown of vitality and where the best spot to begin is. To entangle matters, plant reaction to certain components is species related; not all plants react similarly to a special components. It ought to be recalled that since forever ago, plants have been filling in soils that contain every known component. Those components found in the dirt and in the dirt arrangement in a solvent structure or structures as a particle can be taken into the plant by root retention. This implies that plants will contain most if not each one of those components found in soil. Markert explained what he called the "reference plant structure" of plants, which included 26 components that are not fundamental but rather are found in plants at effectively perceivable focuses? A portion of these components would be classed as "minor components," since they are found in the plant's dry matter at low focuses. This assignment, be that as it may, can prompt some disarray, since the expression "minor components" was once used to recognize what are explained today as the fundamental micronutrients. A portion of these components exist at genuinely high fixations in the plant contingent upon the level of their accessibility in soil.

Kabata-Pendias has given the inexact grouping of 18 insignificant components found in plant leaf tissue, giving their scope of excess to poisonousness to abundance. The inquiry is which of the components, regardless of their discovered con-centration in plants, would contribute, emphatically or adversely, to plant development. An associate and I found that platinum (Pt) at extremely low levels (0.057 mg/L [ppm]) in a hydroponics supplement arrangement invigorated plant development for some plant species, however more significant levels (0.57mg/L ([ppm]) decreased development for all species. The development impacts at the low degree of Pt in arrangement shifted impressively among nine plant species (no reaction: radish and turnip; positive reaction: snap bean, corn, peas, and tomato; negative reaction: broccoli and pepper). It is the "stimulatory impact" of a component that should be researched for those components accessible in soils and soilless media that could be added to a hydroponics supplement arrangement to good plant development. It was perceived by the early analysts that a "total" supplement arrangement ought to incorporate not just the fundamental components known around then yet in addition those that might be good. In this manner, the beginning to end micronutrient arrangement was created. The individuals who may wish to investigate the potential for disclosure of extra components that may demonstrate fundamental for the two creatures and plants will search the books by Mertz and the articles by Asher and Pais intriguing. Four components, Co, Ni, Si, and V, have been concentrated with respect to their possible vitality for plants. Extensive examination has been given to every one of these components, and a few agents feel that they are significant (if not fundamental) components for supporting overwhelming plant development.

Cobalt (Co)

Cobalt is required by implication by leguminous plants since this component is fundamental for the Rhizobium microorganisms that live advantageously in the roots, air nitrogen and giving the host plant a lot of its required N. Without Co, the Rhizobium microscopic organisms are dormant and the vegetable plant at that point requires an inorganic wellspring of N as particles in the dirt arrangement of a fruitful soil. It isn't evident whether the actual plant additionally expects Co to do special biochemical cycles. The incongruity of the connection between Rhizobium microscopic organisms and leguminous plants is that without excess inorganic N in the dirt, which requires the plant to rely entirely upon nitrogen adjusted by the Rhizobium microorganisms, the plant will have all the earmarks of being lack in N, stop to develop, and in the end pass on if Co is absent. Within the sight of satisfactory N in the establishing medium, settlements (knobs) of Rhizobium microbes won't frame on the plant roots.

Silicon (Si)

Plants that are soil developed can contain significant amounts of Si, equivalent in focus (rate levels in the dry make a difference) to that of the significant fundamental components. The majority of the Si ingested (plants can promptly retain silicic corrosive, is saved in the plants as indistinct silica, known as opals. Epstein has recognized six jobs of Si in plants, both physiological and morphological. Inspecting 151 past supplement arrangement details, Hewitt tracked down that a couple of incorporated the component Si. Epstein suggests that Si as sodium silicate be remembered for a Hoagland supplement arrangement plan at 0.25m. Morgan announced that hydroponics preliminaries led in New Zealand brought about yield upgrades for lettuce and bean crops when the Si content in the supplement arrangement was 140 ppm. Ongoing investigations with nursery developed tomato and cucumber have shown that, without excess Si, plants are less fiery and strangely vulnerable to organism illness assault (Belanger et al. 1995). Best development is acquired when the supplement arrangement contains 100 mg/L (ppm) of silicic corrosive. The basic reagent types of Si added to a supplement arrangement are either Na or K silicate, which are dissolvable mixtures, while silicic corrosive is just halfway solvent. Silicon has been discovered to be needed to keep up tail strength in rice and other little grains. Without satisfactory Si in business creation circumstances, these grain plants won't develop upstanding, with housing coming about in great grain misfortune. The issue of housing has been noticed essentially in paddy rice, where soil conditions may influence Si accessibility and take-up. There can be disarray about this component, as the component silicon (Si) often is inappropriately alluded to as silica, which is an insoluble com-pound.

Nickel (Ni)

Nickel is being viewed as a fundamental component for the two vegetables and little grains (i.e., grain), as Brown, Welsh, and Cary and Eskew have shown that its lack prerequisites for centrality set up by Arnon and Stout. Nickel is a segment of the chemical urease, and plants lack in Ni have high aggregations of urea in their leaves. Nickel-lacking plants are moderate developing and, for grain, suitable grain isn't created. It is suggested that a supplement arrangement contain a Ni grouping of in any event 0.057 mg/L (ppm) to fulfill the plant prerequisite for this component, despite the fact that its necessity for other than grain crops has not been set up. Nickel is additionally identified with seed reasonability; its lacking in seed-bearing plants brings about seeds that won't sprout.

Vanadium (V)

Vanadium is by all accounts fit for working as the component Mo in the N digestion of plants, with no free job plainly settled for V. In the event that Mo is at its excess level (its necessity is amazingly low) in the plant, presence and accessibility of V are of no result.

3.7 Element Substitution

There is extensive proof that some trivial components can halfway fill in for a fundamental component, like Na for K, Rb for K, Sr for Ca, and V for Mo. These fractional replacements might be good to plants in circumstances where a fundamental component is at a hardly enough focus. For some plant species, this halfway replacement might be exceptionally good to the plant. In spite of extensive hypothesis, it isn't known precisely how and why such replacements happen, in spite of the fact that comparability in essential qualities (nuclear size and valance) might be the essential factor.

3.8 Visual Plant Symptoms of Elemental Lack or Excess

In the writing, one can search depictions of visual supplement component lack and abundance (poisonous) indications just as photos showing visual manifestations at different phases of plant development. It ought to be recollected that visual manifestations may not show up correspondingly in all plants. In certain examples, on location visual manifestations may not be excessively particular and consequently might be confounding to those new to the strategies of conclusion. To authenticate a presumed lacking, it is alluring to have more than one individual notice the side effects and to present an appropriately gathered plant (leaf) tissue test for essential research facility examination and understanding. Visual manifestations because of basic overabundance are not well recognized for a large number of the fundamental plant supplement components. Some have said that side effects of overabundance are very little not quite the same as those of lack for certain components, especially for a few of the micronutrients. A few components can collect to levels far surpassing their physiological prerequisite yet won't be adverse to the plant. Notwithstanding, it is likewise realized that when a component exists in the plant at a focus a long ways past its physiological prerequisite, such significant levels might be "poisonous" to the plant, meddling with special or general physiological capacities. Harmfulness can likewise happen on the root surface if a component is at an especially high focus in the establishing medium or supplement arrangement washing the roots. An abundance of one component may bring about an unevenness among at least one different components, coming about in a "harmful impact" as far as root capacity and plant development. The consolidated impact of particles in arrangement will change the electrical conductivity (EC) of an answer encompassing the root, or a special ionic equilibrium may adjust the pH of the encompassing arrangement. Along these lines, the entire idea of overabundance can be befuddling because of the differing factors related with high groupings of certain components in the establishing medium or the actual plant. Run of the mill summed up indications of lacking and overabundance are given.

Light green leaf and plant tone; more established leaves become yellow and will ultimately become earthy colored and kick the bucket; plant development is moderate; plants will develop early and be hindered. Plants will be dull green; new development will be delicious; helpless whenever exposed to sickness, bug invasion, and dry season pressure; plants will effectively hold up; bloom fetus removal and absence of natural product set will happen. Plants provided with ammonium nitrogen may display ammonium poisonousness manifestations with starch consumption and decreased plant development; sores may show up on plant stems, alongside descending measuring of leaves; rot of the conductive tissues at the foundations of the stems and shrinking under dampness stress; bloom end organic product decay will happen and Mg lacking side effects may likewise show up. Plant development will be moderate and hindered; more established leaves will have purple hue, especially on the undersides. Abundance manifestations will be visual indications of Zn, Fe, or Mn lacking; high plant P substance may meddle with ordinary Ca nourishment and commonplace Ca lacking side effects may show up. Edges of more established leaves will seem consumed, a side effect known as singe; plants will handily hold up and be touchy to illness invasion; foods grown from the ground creation will be debilitated and of low quality. Plant leaves will show regular Mg and potentially Ca lacking manifestations because of cation irregularity. Developing tips of roots and leaves will become earthy colored and pass on; the edges of leaves will look battered for the edges of arising leaves will remain together; natural product quality will be influenced and bloom end decay will show up on organic products.

Plant leaves may show commonplace Mg lacking indications; in instances of extraordinary overabundance, K lacking may likewise happen. More seasoned leaves will be yellow, with interveinal chlorosis (yellowing between veins) manifestations; development will be moderate and a few plants might be effectively plagued by infection. Result is a cation unevenness with conceivable Ca or K lacking manifestations showing up. Generally light green shade of the whole plant; more seasoned leaves become light green to yellow as the lacking. Untimely senescence of leaves may happen. Unusual advancement of developing points (meristematic tissue); apical developing focuses ultimately become hindered and pass on; blossoms and organic products will cut short; for some grain and natural product harvests, yield and quality are greatly decreased; plant stems might be fragile and effectively break. Leaf tips and edges become earthy colored and pass on. More youthful leaves will be chlorotic and plants will handily wither. Untimely yellowing of the lower leaves with consuming of leaf edges and tips; leaf abscission will happen and plants will effectively wither.

Plant development will be moderate; plants will be hindered; youthful leaves will be misshaped and developing focuses will bite the dust. Iron lacking might be prompted with extremely sluggish development; roots might be hindered. Interveinal chlorosis on arising and youthful leaves with inevitable blanching of the new development; when serious, the whole plant may become light green. Tanning of leaves with little earthy colored spots, a run of the mill indication on certain yields. Interveinal chlorosis of youthful leaves while the leaves and plants remain commonly green; when extreme, the plants will be hindered. More established leaves will show earthy colored spots encompassed by chlorotic zones and circles. Indications are like those of N lacking; more seasoned and center leaves become chlorotic initial and, in certain occurrences, leaf edges are rolled and development and blossom arrangement are limited. Not known and likely not of regular event. Upper leaves will show interveinal chlorosis with brightening of influenced leaves; leaves might be little and misshaped, framing rosettes. Iron lacking side effects will create.

To truly get you all geared up to grow your herbs and vegetables in a hydroponics garden, consider these helpful tips from the experts:

BEST HYDROPONICS HERBS AND VEGETABLES TO PLANT

A lot of herbs can be planted hydroponically on your kitchen window-sill or countertop without taking up too much room. Locating your hydroponics garden in your kitchen is actually a sound idea, considering that it lets you have easy access to the herbs while cooking. Plus, you can rest assured that you will always have an abundant supply of fresh herbs to use for your dishes.

Tip: These herbs are ideally grown in an ebb-flow system or water culture system (you get to plant them in one plant container) if you want to save on kitchen space, although this should not limit you from using other types of hydroponics systems.

1. Basil

Basil is an herb that has the ability for quick growth. It also has the advantage of taking up little space, allowing you to plant plenty of it together with other types of herbs. Basil is best grown using the drip system or NFT system.

2. Chives

Chives lend your baked potatoes great flavor – plant them hydroponically using the ebb-flow or drip system. You can use this garnish as often as you want since it grows quickly and does not require too much maintenance.

3. Oregano

Oregano tastes great with just about any delicious dish, and it certainly goes along very well with pasta, pizza, and paninis. This low-maintenance herb grows best when planted in a drip system or an ebb-flow system.

4. Rosemary

Rosemary is not simply a pretty herb. It gives great aroma and flavor to many meat-based dishes as well as different kinds of breads. You can easily plant rosemary in a drip system, which is ideal for its fibrous root system.

5. Sage

Sage's savory taste, which has a strong hint of pepper, makes it a favorite herb of most chefs. Make it your favorite herb, too – you can easily grow it using the NFT system. If you wish to plant sage along with other herbs, especially if space is an issue, you can always grow it using other types of hydroponics systems as well.

Although it is possible for you to grow almost all kinds of vegetables in your hydroponics garden, you have to keep in mind that some vegetables are more likely to grow in certain hydroponics systems better than others. You also need to address all of your vegetables' other growth requirements besides things that concern hydroponics.

It is also important to remember that whatever system you might use in growing your vegetables hydroponically, you still have to consider the fact that warm-weather vegetables thrive in heat while cool-weather ones do best in low temperatures. It also helps to know that your hydroponics vegetables need lots of sunlight and might require a minimum of eight hours of daily exposure to the sun's rays.

6. Lettuce

Lettuce (Bibb, Romaine, or any other leafy kind) is quite easy to grow hydroponically because it has the ability to thrive even with an extremely simple hydroponics system; plus, it does not require much in terms of maintenance. You can simply harvest your lettuce's outer leaves while it is growing, allowing you to enjoy a continuous supply of fresh and crisp lettuce. You will find that as soon as your lettuce's outer leaves are cut away, they are quickly replaced by the growing inner leaves.

7. Leafy Greens

Most leafy greens are as easy to grow in a hydroponics garden as lettuce. If you plant spinach hydroponically, you will be amazed at how it is not only able to thrive in a soil-less environment; you also get to enjoy harvesting it without all that sandy grit. You can also consider planting other leafy greens in your hydroponics garden such as mustard greens, Swiss chard, arugula, watercress, and kale.

You can choose to harvest your leafy greens by snipping off pieces at a time or all at once. What you should keep in mind when growing leafy greens hydroponically is to avoid letting them grow too big; otherwise, they could suffer from insufficient air circulation.

8. Cucumbers

You will be able to produce lots of bush cucumbers if you plant them in your hydroponics garden, as long as you provide them adequate support as they grow so that they do not tip over. You might consider growing miniature cucumber plants to avoid issues with adequate support and space. It also helps to check on your cucumber plants every day once they start growing; you might be surprised at how much quickly they can grow in a hydroponics system.

9. Root crops

Many of your gardening problems can be easily eliminated with using hydroponics, especially since you will no longer have to deal with any soil-borne-pests or burrowing animals.

This is the reason you should have no second thoughts about growing radishes, beets, turnips, carrots, and other root crops in your hydroponics garden. You might consider using the ebb-flow system to grow your root crops hydroponically – the fact that this system uses as much growing medium as necessary ensures that your plants' growth is supported all the way.

10. Tomato

Hydroponically-grown tomatoes, especially those grown indoors using the drip system, are usually equal to or better than their soil-grown (outdoor) counterparts in terms of nutrition and flavor. This is because these qualities are affected for the most part by temperature and light as well as the nutrients your plants receive as they are growing.

When you grow your tomatoes in a controlled indoor environment, where the plant's nutritional, temperature, and artificial lighting needs are carefully looked after, you enable yourself to harvest them all year long without having to compromise on their flavor and nutritional benefits.

WATERING YOUR HERBS AND VEGETABLES

One of the most important things you have to learn as a beginner in hydroponics gardening is how long as well as how often to water your herbs and vegetables. But trying to know these essentials can be a challenge, especially when you have to consider a number of factors such as the type of growing medium you are using; your hydroponic system's air temperature, water temperature, and humidity levels; and the type and size of your plants, among others.

Fortunately, these tips should be able to help you water your herbs and vegetables properly:

1. Water just long enough so that your growing medium is sufficiently wet, but not too long that your plants' roots end up suffocating from lack of oxygen or air.

2. Water just often enough so that your plants' roots do not dry out. In case you see any wilting, it could mean that your plants are beyond dry or too wet.

3. Keep in mind that the roots of your herbs and vegetables need just the right amount of water for supporting their foliage. This means that the bigger your plants, the more foliage they will have to support, and the more moisture they are going to require. You should also remember that some types of growing media do a better job in holding moisture compared to others, so that they do not require as much watering.

.

Conclusion

This book gives significant data to the business producer, the analyst, the specialist, and the understudy every one of those intrigued by hydroponics and how this strategy for plant creation fills in as applied to a wide scope of developing conditions. Understudies keen on exploring different avenues regarding different hydroponics developing frameworks just as in how to create supplement component lacking in plants are given the required directions.